MILK AND DAIRY

WRITTEN BY E.C. ANDREWS

PowerKiDS press

Published in 2025
by The Rosen Publishing Group, Inc.
2544 Clinton Street, Buffalo, NY 14224

© 2024 BookLife Publishing Ltd.

Written by: E.C. Andrews
Edited by: Elise Carraway
Designed by: Jasmine Pointer

Cataloging-in-Publication Data

Names: Andrews, E.C.
Title: Milk and dairy / E.C. Andrews.
Description: Buffalo, NY : PowerKids Press, 2025. | Series: Fantastic foods | Includes glossary and index.
Identifiers: ISBN 9781499449105 (pbk.) | ISBN 9781499449112 (library bound) | ISBN 9781499449129 (ebook)
Subjects: LCSH: Milk--Juvenile literature. | Dairy products--Juvenile literature.
Classification: LCC TX556.M5 A537 2025 | DDC 641.3'7--dc23

Manufactured in the United States of America
CPSIA Compliance Information: Batch #CW25PK. For further information contact Rosen Publishing at 1-800-237-9932.

Find us on

Image Credits
All images are courtesy of Shutterstock.com. With thanks to Getty Images, Thinkstock Photo and iStockphoto.
Cover – Anton Starikov, Atsushi Hirao, MaraZe, Tanya Sid, Spalnic, iKatod.
4–5 – Ixepop, Goskova Tatiana.
6–7 – Dedy_SW, Birkir Asgeirsson.
8–9 – margouillat photo, New Africa. 10–11 – David Evison, MaraZe, Tomo Bagaric. 12–13 – New Africa, WS-Studio, Ahanov Michael. 14–15 – grey_and, Santhosh Varghese, gresei.
16–17 – Artem Oleshko, Umomos. 18–19 – Kitreel, VanderWolf Images.
20–21 – Pixel-Shot, Tatjana Baibakova. 22–23 – NDAB Creativity, New Africa.

CONTENTS

Words that look like this can be found in the glossary on page 24.

DAILY DIET

Do you know what dairy is? Do you know where dairy comes from or how it ends up in your food? You might be wondering why it matters. You eat enough food to feel full, right?

What's in your food is important. You need to eat the right amounts of different things. This is called eating a balanced diet. A balanced diet can include milk and dairy. Let's discover why!

WHAT IS MILK?

We cannot talk about dairy without first understanding what milk is. Milk is a white <u>liquid</u> that is made in the bodies of <u>mammals</u>. Milk can be drunk on its own or made into food.

A lot of the milk that humans use comes from cows. However, some foods are made using goat milk or buffalo milk. Each kind of milk has a different taste.

WHAT IS DAIRY?

Foods that are made using milk are called dairy products. Cream, cheese, butter, and yogurt are all dairy products. Dairy is also used in some sweet foods, such as cheesecake, milk chocolate, and ice cream.

Many dairy products are a good <u>source</u> of protein. Protein helps your body grow. Protein helps your <u>muscles</u> fix themselves when they need to. Milk also has calcium in it. Calcium helps keep your bones strong.

CREAM

Cream is something that comes from milk. When fresh milk is left to stand, fatty cream rises to the top of it. People separate the cream from the milk to use it for different things.

When air is mixed into cream, it can become thicker and lighter. This is called whipped cream. You might have had whipped cream with hot chocolate as a treat. Cream is also used to cook with.

Some sauces are made with cream.

BUTTER

Butter is a food that starts out as cream. To make butter, the cream is churned. This means it is shaken and stirred up. Churning cream causes the fat to clump together. This makes butter.

Butter is used for lots of different things. You can put it on toast or sandwiches. Butter is often used for making sauces. Baked goods, like cakes and cookies, often have butter in them.

YOGURT

Yogurt is a food made by heating and fermenting milk. Yogurt is thicker than milk and tastes sourer. Yogurt has less fat than cream and can have lots of different flavors added to it.

Eating yogurt with fruit can make a healthy, delicious breakfast. Yogurt can also be eaten as a healthy snack during the day. It is sometimes eaten with spicy foods to make them feel less hot.

CHEESE

Cheese is made from milk that has been fermented. Fermenting milk makes cheese last longer than most other dairy products. The fermented milk becomes chunky and separates into <u>curds</u> and <u>whey</u>. The curds are then cooked.

Salt is added to the curds, which dries them out, stops bacteria and adds flavor. The cheese is then complete. There are many kinds of cheese. Cheese can be eaten on its own or with other foods.

Where Do MILK and DAIRY Come From?

Milk comes from living things. So, it is important to make sure we get our milk and dairy from places that treat animals well. Buying dairy from <u>local</u> farms might be a good place to start.

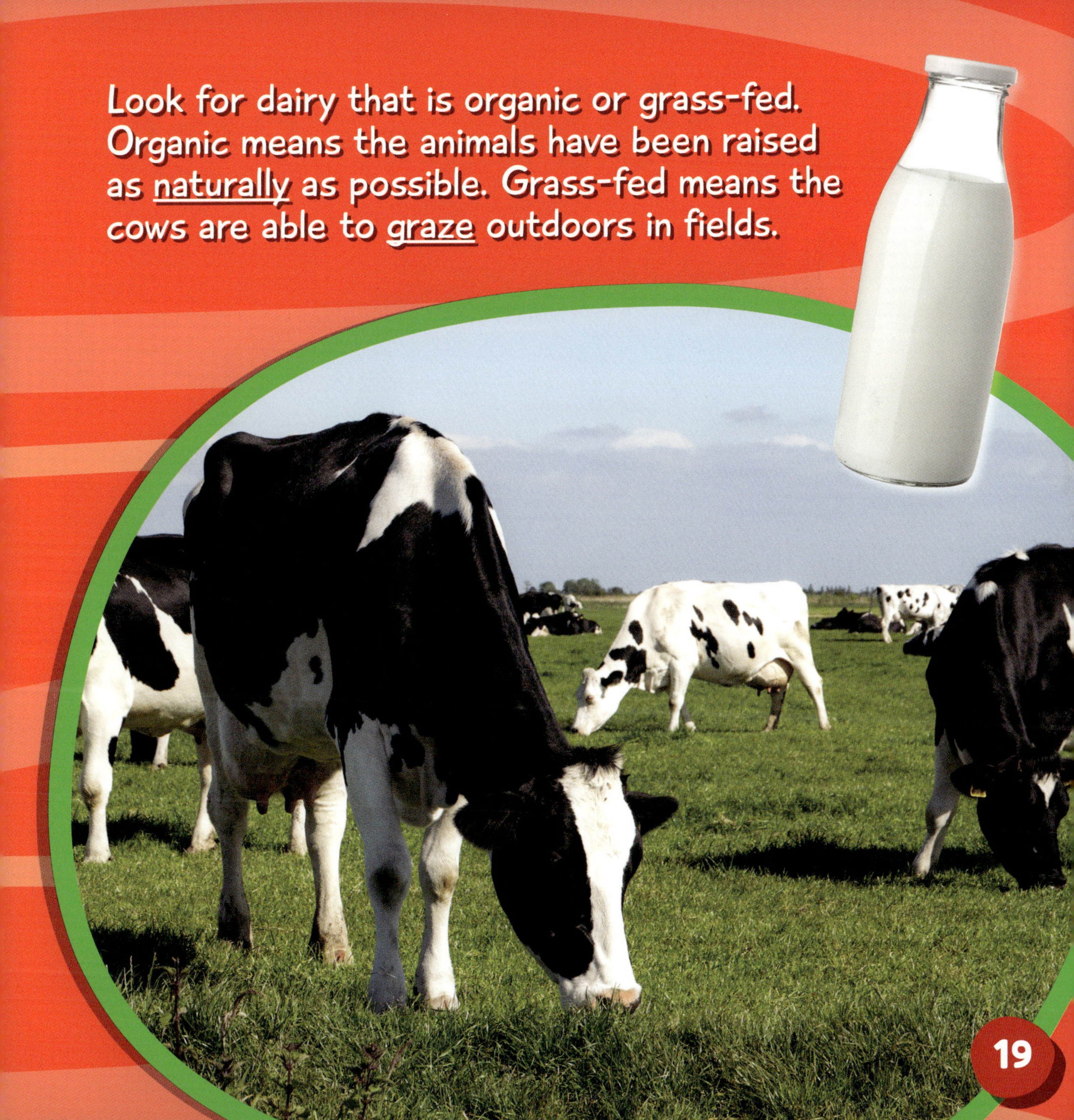

Look for dairy that is organic or grass-fed. Organic means the animals have been raised as <u>naturally</u> as possible. Grass-fed means the cows are able to <u>graze</u> outdoors in fields.

19

CALCIUM in Other FOODS

Calcium is an important part of a balanced diet. Calcium helps keep our bones strong. However, not everyone drinks milk or eats dairy. Some people cannot, as it makes them sick. Calcium can be found in other foods.

Dairy-free milks, such as oat, almond, rice, and hazelnut milk, do not come from animals. They all have different amounts of calcium in them. You can also find calcium in eggs, tofu, broccoli, almonds, and kale.

PERFECT PLATE

If you are able to eat dairy, it can be a great source of calcium and protein. But remember, you also need other types of food to keep your diet balanced.

Here are some of the different kinds of foods that can be eaten alongside milk and dairy as part of a balanced diet.

GLOSSARY

bacteria — tiny living things that are too small to see

curds — soft, white clumps that come from separated milk

graze — to eat grass in a field

liquid — a material that flows, such as water

local — having to do with the nearby area

mammals — animals that are warm-blooded, have a backbone, and produce milk to feed their young

muscles — the parts of the body that allow for movement

naturally — having to do with how things are in nature and not affected by humans

source — where something comes from

whey — the watery part of milk that separates from lumpy bits called curds

INDEX